The Richest Man in Manhattan

A Modern Retelling of George S. Clason's The Richest Man in Babylon

L.B.A Tolkings

Summit House Publishers

Chicago IL

The Richest Man in Manhattan

This is a work of fiction. Any resemblance to actual persons, living or dead, or actual events is purely coincidental. While inspired by The Richest Man in Babylon by George S. Clason, this book is an original modern retelling and not affiliated with or endorsed by the estate of George S. Clason.

First Edition

ISBN: 978-1-7356699-8-4

Published by: Summit House Publishers

http://.summitpublishers.com

For permissions, speaking engagements, and bulk orders, contact:

info@summipublishers.com

Printed in the United States of America

Contents

Dedication

To those who seek timeless wisdom,

To those who believe the past holds the key to the future,

And to everyone ready to take control of their financial journey,

This book is for you.

Acknowledgments

Every journey worth taking is never walked alone—and this book is no exception.

To the Original Voice: *The Richest Man in Babylon* by George S. Clason was the seed. Your timeless wisdom planted something in me years ago, and this retelling is my way of watering that seed for a new generation.

To those who live in stories: Ben, Sam, and Arkad may be fictional, but they are stitched together from the voices, struggles, and breakthroughs of so many real people I've met—friends, students, family, clients, and dreamers. You showed me what transformation looks like, and I tried to honor your journey here.

To my mentors and teachers: Thank you for teaching me that true wealth begins not in the wallet, but in the mind and spirit. Your lessons echo through every chapter.

To my family—those I live for and those I love deeply: Thank you for your constant support, your laughter in the chaos, and your faith in my calling. You are my wealth.

To the readers: You are the reason this story exists. Whether you're reading these words on a subway in the city, late at night at your kitchen table, or with hope tucked between pages—I honor your hunger for growth. My deepest hope is that this book sparks something in you, something courageous and new.

And above all, to the One who gives power to get wealth, and teaches our hands to build what truly matters—thank You.

Here's to the journey.

— L. B. A. Tolkings

Epigraph

"The lessons of wealth are timeless. Whether in ancient Babylon or modern Manhattan, the principles remain the same—save, invest, and grow."

— Inspired by The Richest Man in Babylon

Introduction: A Modern Retelling of Timeless Wisdom

Nearly a century ago, George S. Clason wrote The Richest Man in Babylon, a collection of parables that revealed the timeless principles of wealth building. His stories, set in the golden streets of ancient Babylon, taught readers the importance of saving, investing, living within their means, and using money as a tool to achieve freedom and purpose.

This book, The Richest Man in Manhattan, is a modern retelling of those principles. It transports the timeless lessons of Babylon to the bustling streets of Manhattan, a city that embodies ambition, opportunity, and financial complexity.

Through the story of Ben and Sam, you'll see how the same principles that built fortunes in Babylon can help navigate the challenges of today's fast-paced world. This is not merely a guide to wealth—it's a story of growth, transformation, and the enduring power of wisdom to shape our lives.

If you've ever felt that financial freedom is out of reach, this book is here to remind you: the path has always been the same. It begins with small steps, consistent habits, and the willingness to learn.

Welcome to your journey of rediscovery.

Chapter One

Living for Payday

The sun was setting over Manhattan, casting a golden glow upon the towers that reached for the heavens. From a distance, the city looked eternal, like a monument to human ambition. But inside, beneath the gleam and bustle, lived people carrying silent questions in their hearts.

The aroma of roasted beans mingled with the metallic scent of the city. A street saxophonist played a melody that sounded like longing, and in a small café on Lexington Avenue—sheltered between glass buildings that mirrored the sky—two friends sat in a quiet corner, lost in thought.

Ben loosened his tie as though the day itself had wrapped too tightly around his neck. He stared into his coffee as if it might contain an answer. "I don't understand it, Sam," he said. "I'm making more money than I ever have, yet every month feels like a race I lose at the finish line."

Sam nodded. His hands were ink-stained from sketches. He was a creator, a dreamer, a man juggling projects and payments like spinning plates.

"Same here. I had two big clients last month. Checks came in yesterday. I paid the rent, threw some money at the credit card, and now I'm back where I started. It's like this city consumes everything I give it."

Ben chuckled bitterly.

"Welcome to Manhattan. Where the lights are bright, the rents are brutal, and your savings don't stand a chance."

Sam smirked. "Savings? I don't have savings. I have a cycle."

Their words drifted into the warm air of the café, blending with laughter, the hum of conversation, and the faint jazz from the street. For a moment, neither spoke. But their silence wasn't empty—it was searching.

Ben finally spoke again, his voice quieter now. "Do you remember Arkad?"

Sam's eyes lit with recognition. "Money Man Arkad? From college?"

Ben nodded. "Yeah. Always selling something. Books, tutoring, side gigs. We used to tease him, remember? Said he was obsessed with money."

Sam laughed. "He was. Always talking about 'cracking the code.'"

"Well," Ben said, "it looks like he did. He's living in Tribeca now. Works when he wants. Travels. Parties on rooftops. He was once broke like us—but now, he's not."

Sam leaned back in his chair, folding his arms. "So what changed? Did he get lucky?"

Ben shook his head slowly. "I don't believe in luck like that. Not the kind that moves someone from ramen noodles to rooftop lofts. He knows something. Something we never learned."

He paused. "And I want to ask him."

Sam raised an eyebrow. "Ask? You think he'd just tell us?"

Ben looked out the café window at the lights flickering on in the towers above them.

"Why not? Sometimes the journey begins with a question."

They pulled out their phones, searching through old contacts. Sam found Arkad's number and sent a message. Neither expected a reply that night. But both felt something shift—something small but undeniable. As if a door had opened, not in the city, but in their minds.

They stepped back out onto the sidewalk. The streetlights had come alive, painting halos on the pavement. The saxophonist played on, and the crowd moved like a river.

Ben looked up at the skyline. "You ever feel like those skyscrapers? Like you were made to rise, but somehow you're stuck, always looking up?

Sam smirked, hands in his coat pockets. "That's deep for a guy with no savings."

Ben smiled faintly. "Maybe that changes soon."

As they disappeared into the city's rhythm, their footsteps joined the music of Manhattan. The night didn't offer answers—only direction.

Somewhere above them, a man named Arkad had unlocked a secret. A simple one, yet so easily missed.

A secret anyone could follow, but few ever did.

Financial Principle:

> ***Many chase paychecks; few pursue wisdom.***
>
> *True wealth does not begin with more income, but with a clearer understanding. The journey begins the moment you choose to ask—gently, boldly, and with an open heart.*

Discussion Guide

1. Chapter Summary

Set against the backdrop of a restless Manhattan evening, this chapter introduces Ben and Sam—two friends navigating success without security. Though both are talented and working professionals, they find themselves stuck in a financial cycle that leaves them frustrated and empty. Their conversation sparks a turning point: the decision to seek out Arkad, a former college acquaintance who seems to have cracked the code of true wealth. This chapter reminds us that transformation often begins not with answers, but with the courage to ask the right questions.

2. Key Quote

"Sometimes the journey begins with a question."

3. Reflection Questions

- What emotions or thoughts came up as you read about Ben and Sam's experiences?
- Have you ever felt like you were earning well but going nowhere financially? What contributed to that feeling?
- Why do you think most people, like Ben and Sam, wait so long before asking for help or seeking financial wisdom?
- What does the quote "Many chase paychecks; few pursue wisdom" mean to you personally?

4. Personal Action Steps

- Identify one financial struggle or cycle you're currently facing. Write it down clearly.
- Think of one person you admire for their financial wisdom or lifestyle. Consider reaching out to them with a thoughtful question.
- Take one small step to begin your own journey toward financial clarity—whether it's reading a book, starting a journal, or tracking your spending this week.

5. Group Discussion Questions

- How does our culture shape the way we think about money,

success, and "making it"?

- What role does comparison play in how we measure our financial progress?
- Why do you think it's so hard to talk openly about money with others? How can we change that in our own communities?

Chapter Two

The Wealthbuilder's First Gift of Self-Love

The next evening, Ben and Sam stood at the foot of a building that seemed to whisper of other lives—lives not trapped by rent cycles and silent worries. The building gleamed in the last light of day, its glass exterior reflecting the gold of the setting sun. It was everything success seemed to look like in Manhattan—modern, elegant, and inaccessible to most.

They exchanged glances that mixed curiosity with disbelief.

"This is where Arkad lives?" Sam asked, eyeing the chandelier inside the lobby.

Ben smirked as he pressed the elevator button. "Either that, or we're about to get arrested for impersonating people who belong here."

As the elevator rose, so did their anticipation. When the doors opened to the 18th floor, they stepped into a hallway lined with abstract art and quiet luxury. At the end, Arkad's door stood slightly open. Music spilled into the corridor—a soft jazz tune, smooth as velvet.

Ben knocked lightly.

"Ben. Sam."Arkad's voice echoed like a song you hadn't heard in years—but instantly recognized. He stepped into view, barefoot on polished floors, wearing a soft charcoal sweater and jeans that looked like they cost more than a week's rent—but wore them like old memories.

He smiled wide, arms open. "It's really you. I thought maybe my past was playing tricks on me."

He hugged them both—firmly, like someone who had learned that time is short and friends are treasures.

"Come in, before the city charges you for standing still," he laughed.

The apartment greeted them with quiet elegance. Light spilled through floor-to-ceiling windows like golden syrup, washing over furniture that seemed both expensive and lived-in. The skyline stretched endlessly, a reminder of dreams too big for ceilings.

Sam whistled. "This place is unreal. It's like the sky decided to live indoors."

Arkad waved it off. "It's just a room with a view. But I've learned that when your mind expands, your space follows."

They sat on a velvet-gray sectional that seemed to mold to their fatigue.

"So," Arkad said, his eyes kind and clear, "tell me. What brings two wanderers of Wall Street and Wi-Fi to my little nest in the clouds? You finally selling your souls to Silicon Valley?"

Ben chuckled. "Not yet. We're just... stuck. We work hard, we earn more than we ever have, but we're always scraping by. Meanwhile, you're up here, sipping skyline like it's coffee. What's your secret?"

Arkad didn't answer right away. He simply looked at them—really looked—and his silence said more than any clever reply.

The First Lesson

Arkad leaned back, thoughtful.

"It's not a secret," he said at last. "It's a principle. And most people miss it because it's not flashy."

Ben leaned forward. "We're listening."

"Pay yourself first," Arkad said simply.

Sam frowned. "I've heard that before. Sounds like something from a YouTube motivational ad."

Arkad nodded. "That's because truth echoes. You just have to decide whether you'll listen or scroll past."

Ben raised an eyebrow. "So what does it actually mean?"

"It means this: From every dollar you earn, you set aside a portion—at least ten percent—for yourself. Before rent. Before coffee.

Before groceries. Before Netflix. Before the world takes a piece of you, you take one for your future."

Sam crossed his arms. "Sounds great. But this is Manhattan. Ten percent feels like a luxury.

Arkad smiled. "Manhattan isn't the problem. It's not what you earn—it's what you keep. People find money for brunch, for shoes, for subscriptions they forgot about. The issue isn't money—it's mindset."

Ben nodded slowly. "So... start with ten percent. Always."

"Exactly. And don't just let it sit. Invest it. Make it work. Turn every dollar into an employee. Most people spend first and save what's left. But those who build wealth save first—and spend with intention."

The Challenge

Arkad rose and walked to a shelf, retrieving three slim notebooks.

"These are for you," he said, handing one to each of them. "For the next 30 days, track every dollar. Write it down. Not just the big stuff—everything. And at the same time, save at least five percent of what you earn. Ten, if you can."

Sam opened his notebook, flipping through the empty pages.

"And then what?"

Arkad's eyes sparkled. "Then we meet again. And I'll show you what to do with the seeds you've planted."

As They Left

Back on the bustling Manhattan sidewalk, the air felt cooler, but their minds were burning with possibility. The buildings didn't look so distant anymore. They looked like something that could be built, one stone at a time.

Ben glanced up and whispered, more to himself than anyone else:

"Maybe wealth doesn't start with riches. Maybe it starts with a shift."

Sam smiled. "And maybe ten percent is the price of believing in yourself."

Financial Principle:

> ***Pay yourself first.***
>
> *A part of all you earn is yours to keep.*
>
> *Let it be the first act of love you give yourself in a world that tries to take everything. From that small act, something beautiful begins to grow.*
>
> *Set aside at least 10% of every dollar you earn. In time, this habit becomes a foundation—quiet but sure—on which wealth is built.*

Discussion Guide

1. Chapter Summary

Ben and Sam meet Arkad for the first time in years. His rooftop apartment overlooking the city is a world away from the financial struggles they're facing. Instead of launching into investment tips or side hustles,

Arkad begins with something deeper: *the principle of paying yourself first.* He tells them that true wealth-building starts by honoring your future self—saving consistently before spending. It's a shift from chasing more money to mastering how money flows through your life.

2. Key Quote

> "Before the world takes a piece of you, you take one for your future."

3. Reflection Questions

- What does the phrase "pay yourself first" mean to you beyond just saving money?
- How does the concept of honoring your future self affect your current spending habits?
- In what ways have you been paying others (landlords, lenders, etc.) before paying yourself?
- What excuses or obstacles have you faced that prevent you from consistently saving?

4. Personal Action Steps

- Commit to setting aside at least 10% of your income, starting with your next paycheck—even if it's a small amount.

- Write down your top three long-term financial dreams (e.g., freedom, travel, security, generosity).
- Create a simple "Wealth Jar" or a separate savings account to symbolize your new commitment to your future.

5. Group Discussion Questions

- Why do you think the principle of paying yourself first is often ignored, even by high earners?
- How can we reshape our conversations around savings to make it feel like empowerment, not deprivation?
- What role does consistency play in wealth building, and why is it more powerful than intensity?
- If everyone in your group practiced this principle for one year, what changes would you expect to see?

Chapter Three

The Money That Never Sleeps

Ben and Sam returned to Arkad's apartment in Tribeca as the evening sun dipped below the skyline. The marble floor of the lobby gleamed beneath soft lights, and the elevator's familiar chime greeted them like an old friend.

They weren't the same men who had arrived here weeks ago. They carried something new with them—not just notebooks, but understanding.

Arkad opened the door with a grin. "Let's see what the past month has taught you."

They settled into the living room, now a space that felt more like a classroom than a luxury apartment.

Ben opened his notebook and flipped through its worn pages. "Tracking my spending changed everything. I didn't realize how casually I spent money on little things. They weren't purchases—they were leaks."

Sam nodded. "I started saving 10%, and once I got past the discomfort, I pushed it to 12%. It was like choosing between who I was and who I wanted to become."

Arkad clapped his hands. "Beautiful. You've passed the first gate. Now comes the second: learning to let your money do what it was made to do."

Let Money Work While You Rest

Ben leaned forward. "What do you mean—'work for me'?"

Arkad turned toward the window. The city pulsed below.

"Every dollar," he said, "is a little worker. If you let them rest, they sit idly in the shadows of your bank account. But if you give them purpose, they labor for you. Quietly. Faithfully. Even while you sleep."

Sam furrowed his brow. "You mean investing?"

"Yes," Arkad replied. "But not blind gambling. Investing is choosing where your workers go and ensuring their work is profitable. A poor investment is like hiring someone who eats lunch all day. They promise results but cost you in the end."

Lessons Written in Loss

Arkad leaned back and let out a chuckle. "When I first saved money, I gave it to a friend who had an exciting idea. 'Double your money in six months,' he promised. He had energy but no plan. I lost it all."

Ben winced. "Ouch."

Arkad smiled. "It was the price of my first real education. Since then, I don't send my money where I wouldn't go myself. I learned to ask questions. To read. To think."

Sam tilted his head. "So where did you start, really?"

"I began with index funds—simple, steady, and patient. Then I bought a small property uptown. One decision built upon another, and suddenly I wasn't the one working hardest anymore. My money was."

The Gentle Power of Time

He reached for a tablet and opened a chart of compound growth. The line rose slowly at first, then climbed higher with grace.

"This," he said, "is the secret people overlook. Time. If you invest $100 every month, starting now, you could have over $70,000 in 20 years. But if you delay ten years before starting, you'll have less than half by the same age."

Ben stared at the numbers. "So time multiplies effort."

Arkad nodded. "It is your quietest ally. The one who waits for you—but not forever."

The First Step into the Field

"So where should we begin?" Sam asked. "We've saved, but it's not much."

"You begin," Arkad said, "by planting what's in your hand. If you've saved $500, consider a diversified ETF. If real estate calls to you, look into REITs. The point is not to have much, but to start with what you have."

Ben hesitated. "What if we mess up again?"

"You will," Arkad said with a warm laugh. "But mistakes can be tutors if you let them. Never risk more than you can afford to lose, and never stop learning."

The Next Assignment

He handed them each a single sheet of paper.

"Your new task," he said, "is to invest. Research. Choose something that feels right to you—not based on hype, but on understanding. Next time we meet, we won't just talk about what you did. We'll talk about what it taught you."

Sam looked at the page. "Still feels big."

Arkad placed a hand on his shoulder. "Big things always do. Until they are behind you."

A City of Possibility

As Ben and Sam stepped back into the Manhattan night, the city lights blinked like stars caught in steel and glass. The crowd moved fast, but they walked slower—more deliberate.

"You think we can really do this?" Ben asked.

Sam smiled. "We already are. This time, our money's not just sitting in our pockets. It's going to work."

Ben chuckled. "Here's to night shifts we don't have to show up for."

They walked on. Quietly richer already.

Financial Principle:

Make your money work for you.

Every dollar is a worker. Train them, assign them wisely, and let time be their supervisor. Wealth grows while you sleep—if your workers are on the clock.

Discussion Guide

1. Chapter Summary

Ben and Sam return to Arkad's apartment for their next lesson. They've begun to save, and now Arkad teaches them that saving is just the beginning—true wealth is built when your money works for you. Through personal stories, practical advice, and the power of time, Arkad introduces them to the world of investing and the mindset of ownership.

2. Key Quote

> "Every dollar is a little worker... Quietly. Faithfully.
> Even while you sleep."

3. Reflection Questions

- What has been your view of investing up until now? Has it seemed intimidating or empowering?
- Arkad says, "Never send your money where you wouldn't go yourself." What does this mean to you, and how could it affect your decisions?

- Time is described as your "quietest ally." How can starting early change your financial future?
- What lessons have you learned from past financial missteps?

4. Personal Action Steps

- Identify one area where your money is idle and explore a way to put it to work (e.g., savings account to investment account).
- Spend one hour researching a simple investment vehicle (e.g., ETFs, REITs, index funds).
- Choose one small amount (e.g., $50–$500) you could invest this month—and create a plan to do so.
- Write out a list of financial "workers" (dollars) and where you want to assign them over the next year.

5. Group Discussion Questions

- Why do many people save but never invest?
- What fears or misconceptions stop people from letting their money work for them?
- How can accountability with others (like Ben and Sam have with Arkad) make the investing journey more successful?
- Investment vehicles tried. What worked, and didn't?

Chapter Four

The Subtle Thief

Three months had passed, and with it, a shift had taken root in Ben and Sam. They returned to Arkad's Tribeca apartment not as novices, but as men who had dipped their toes into unfamiliar waters and discovered they could swim.

Ben had chosen a diversified ETF. Sam had invested in a REIT. Their portfolios were still small, but they were no longer idle. Their money had begun its quiet labor.

Arkad welcomed them like an old friend. "Come in, come in. What stories have your dollars written since we last met?"

Ben's face lit up. "It's growing, Arkad. Slowly—but it's real."

Sam added, "It's steady for me too. But I'll admit, I keep thinking about pulling some of it out to buy something nice."

Arkad chuckled knowingly. "Ah, yes. That voice. It sounds like a reward but often turns out to be a robber. Today, we must talk about a silent danger—one that has ruined many who looked wealthy but were actually poor."

The Subtle Thief of Wealth

"Lifestyle inflation," Arkad said, settling into his chair, "is the thief that never knocks. It slips in quietly, dressed as progress. You earn more, so you spend more. You justify it. After all, you deserve it."

Ben leaned forward. "Like buying a nicer place, a newer car... just because you can?"

"Exactly," Arkad said. "I made that mistake too. When my income rose, so did my lifestyle. I moved to a nicer apartment. Bought designer clothes. Took fancy vacations. I felt successful. But when I checked my accounts, I realized—I was still broke. Just broke at a higher level."

The Illusion of More

Sam furrowed his brow. "But what's the point of making money if you can't enjoy it?"

"It's not about denial," Arkad said. "It's about discipline. Joy is not in reckless spending—it's in intentional living. You can reward yourself, but do it with wisdom. Let your life reflect growth, not just gloss."

Ben tapped his pen against his notebook. "So we're not saying no to pleasure—we're saying yes to a better kind of pleasure. One that lasts."

Arkad nodded. "Well said. When you let your money grow, you don't just buy things. You buy time. Freedom. Options. You're not just living for today—you're building for tomorrow."

Breaking the Cycle

"So how do we keep ourselves from falling into this?" Sam asked.

"Simple," Arkad said. "Live beneath your means, even when your means increase. When you get a raise, don't rush to upgrade your lifestyle. Upgrade your investments. Give your dollars more workers to manage, not more bills to pay."

He smiled, tapping his temple. "If you control your desires, you control your destiny."

Ben scribbled furiously. "I was thinking about moving to a bigger apartment. But maybe it's not time yet."

"A bigger space doesn't mean a better life," Arkad said. "But a bigger margin between income and expenses? That creates room for dreams."

The Rule of Gratitude

"There's something else," Arkad added. "Gratitude."

He paused.

"When you learn to appreciate what you already have, you're not as quick to chase what you don't. In this city, comparison is currency. Everyone's showing off something. But true wealth doesn't perform. It prepares."

Sam leaned back, a thoughtful expression on his face. "So we're not just saving money. We're saving ourselves—from the pressure to impress, from the race we never signed up for."

Arkad nodded. "Exactly. Contentment is a quiet superpower."

A New Challenge

Arkad handed them each a single sheet of paper—another challenge.

"This time," he said, "your task isn't just about what you earn or save. It's about how you spend. Track every unnecessary purchase you're tempted to make this month. And each time, ask: Is this helping or hurting my future?"

Ben smiled. "Time to give every dollar a background check."

Sam laughed. "Guess I'll rethink that trip to Miami."

A Walk with New Eyes

They walked through the glowing streets of Manhattan, past the glass towers and neon dreams. But something had changed.

Where they once saw temptations, they now saw trade-offs.

Where they once felt envy, they now felt clarity.

Ben looked up at a billboard advertising luxury watches. "You know, I used to think that wealth meant having more stuff."

Sam grinned. "Now I think it means needing less."

Ben nodded. "Here's to keeping our workers on the job—and our future in focus."

Financial Principle:

> ***Beware the silent thief of lifestyle inflation.***
> *Live below your means—especially as your means grow. Every dollar you save today is a brick in the foundation of your future freedom.*

Discussion Guide

1. Chapter Summary

Ben and Sam return to Arkad's apartment three months into their financial transformation. Having made their first investments, they're eager to grow—but Arkad warns them of a hidden danger: lifestyle inflation. This chapter explores the temptation to increase spending with income and reveals the deeper satisfaction found in discipline, gratitude, and intentional living.

2. Key Quote

> "A bigger space doesn't mean a better life. But a bigger margin between income and expenses? That creates room for dreams."

3. Reflection Questions

- When have you personally experienced the temptation of lifestyle inflation? How did it affect your finances?
- What do you think Arkad means by "comparison is currency" in a city like Manhattan?
- In your own words, how does gratitude protect against overspending?
- Can you identify an area where "more" has not brought you greater peace or purpose?

4. Personal Action Steps

- Set a cap for your lifestyle spending—even as your income increases.
- List three recent purchases you made to "reward" yourself. Would you make those same choices again today?
- Write out a simple lifestyle upgrade plan: what is truly essential, what's occasional, and what's unnecessary?
- Track every non-essential purchase you feel tempted to make this month. Journal your thought process before and after the decision.

5. Group Discussion Questions

- Why do you think lifestyle inflation is so difficult to notice in real time?
- How can a community of friends (like Ben and Sam) help keep each other financially grounded?
- What cultural messages feed the desire to "look rich," and how can we resist them?
- What role does gratitude play in financial maturity—and how do we cultivate it?

Chapter Five

The Wealth of Wisdom

Ben and Sam returned to Arkad's Tribeca apartment for their next lesson, notebooks in hand and a month of self-reflection behind them. They had worked hard—cutting back on spending, resisting lifestyle inflation, and even increasing their savings rates. But despite their progress, a new realization had settled in:

There was still so much they didn't know.

As they stepped into the apartment, Arkad welcomed them with a grin. "Ah, my faithful students! I hope you've been keeping your workers busy and not firing them too soon."

Ben chuckled. "We're trying. But honestly, we've hit a wall. The more we learn, the more we realize how much we don't know—investments, taxes, planning for the future. It's overwhelming."

Sam nodded in agreement. "We're not even sure where to start anymore."

Arkad's smile softened. "Then today's lesson will be timely. It's not just about saving and investing—it's about *understanding*. Wealth without wisdom is like a car with no steering wheel. Let's talk about growing your financial literacy."

The Importance of Knowledge

He motioned them to the couch and handed each of them a small stack of books—*The Bible, The Simple Path to Wealth*, *Rich Dad Poor Dad*, *The Psychology of Money*, and a few others.

"Knowledge," Arkad said, "is your greatest asset. No one is born understanding money—it's a skill, like cooking or driving. The good news? Anyone can learn it."

Ben flipped through a few pages. "But how do you know what's actually worth learning? There's so much noise—everyone online has an opinion."

"That's where principles come in," Arkad replied. "Focus on timeless truths. Learn the basics: how to budget, how to invest, how taxes work, how to avoid bad debt. Once you understand these pillars, the rest becomes easier to filter."

Learning from Mentors

"Books are great," Arkad said, "but they're just the beginning. Mentorship accelerates mastery."

Sam looked up. "What if we don't know anyone who's actually good with money?"

"Then find them," Arkad replied. "Attend workshops. Join communities. Look online for forums or podcasts. You'll be surprised how generous successful people are when they sense your sincerity."

Ben nodded. "So it's not just about reading—it's about positioning yourself to grow."

"Exactly. Watch what people do, not just what they say. Ask questions. Stay curious. Surround yourself with wisdom, and it will change you."

Avoiding the Pitfalls of Ignorance

Arkad leaned back, recalling a lesson of his own. "Years ago, I invested in a startup because a friend promised it would double my money in three months. I didn't understand the business. I didn't ask enough questions."

Sam winced. "You lost it?"

"Every dollar. But that loss taught me more than most of my wins: Never invest in something you don't understand."

Ben scribbled that down. "So, the goal is to become a student of money?"

Arkad nodded. "Absolutely. Not just for a season—for life. The more you learn, the wiser your decisions become. Financial ignorance is expensive. Knowledge pays dividends."

A Practical Challenge

He handed them a printed checklist titled: *The Wealth Builder's Learning Plan*.

"This month, pick one area that confuses you—stocks, taxes, retirement planning, real estate. Study it. Read a book. Watch a course. Talk to someone who knows more than you. And most importantly, write down what you learn."

Ben scanned the paper. "Should we try applying it?"

"Yes," Arkad said. "But start small. Apply your learning in manageable ways. Build your confidence before you build your empire."

The Walk Back

Manhattan buzzed as they stepped back into the rhythm of the city, but this time, their minds were more alive than their senses. The lights still dazzled, but their focus had shifted from what could be bought to what could be built.

"You know," Sam said, "I always thought money was something you just *had* or didn't. I never thought of it as something you *study*."

Ben smiled. "But that's what Arkad's been teaching us. Wealth isn't a mystery—it's a subject. And we're finally starting to learn the language."

"Let's just hope we pass the test," Sam joked.

"We will," Ben said. "Because now we know to keep learning."

Financial Principle:

> ***Grow your financial knowledge.***
> *Read, ask questions, and learn from those who have succeeded. The more you understand, the better your decisions will be—and the wealthier your future will become.*

Discussion Guide

1. Chapter Summary

In this chapter, Ben and Sam recognize a new obstacle on their journey: ignorance. They've made progress in saving and resisting lifestyle inflation, but feel unequipped to handle more complex topics like taxes, investments, and financial planning. Arkad introduces the idea that wealth-building is a skill—one that must be studied like any other discipline. Through books, mentorship, and intentional learning, they begin to grasp the value of growing financial literacy as a lifelong pursuit.

2. Key Quote

Wealth without wisdom is like a car with no steering wheel."

3. Reflection Questions

- What's one area of your financial life that still confuses or overwhelms you?
- How have you grown (or not grown) in your financial understanding over the past year?
- What has been your biggest money mistake—and what did you learn from it?
- Do you have a mentor or trusted source of financial wisdom in your life? If not, how might you find one?

4. Personal Action Steps

- Identify one financial topic you struggle with (e.g. investing, budgeting, taxes).
- Choose a book, podcast, course, or mentor to explore that topic in depth this month.

- Start a financial learning journal—write down key takeaways, questions, and next steps.
- Take one small action to apply your learning—open an account, adjust a budget, or research a financial tool.

5. Group Discussion Questions

- Why do you think financial literacy isn't taught more widely or emphasized in schools?
- What are some "timeless truths" about money that have helped you make better decisions?
- How can accountability and community support help you stay committed to learning about money?
- In what ways does increasing knowledge lead to financial confidence—and how can we sustain that growth over time?

Chapter Six

Breaking the Chains

The night air in Tribeca carried a bite, like the city itself was whispering truths they were finally ready to face.

Ben and Sam walked slower than usual, as if their feet were tethered to memories they could no longer ignore. The progress had been real—budgeting, saving, investing. Yet, under every good decision lay a shadow.

Debt.

They entered Arkad's warm apartment, but the weight they carried did not stay at the door.

"You walk like men dragging ghosts behind you," Arkad said, motioning them in. "What burden lingers tonight?"

Ben sank into the couch. "Debt. It follows me, even in sleep. I've started saving, but the moment I pause, I feel it—student loans, credit cards—like quicksand around my ankles."

Sam nodded. "I'm working harder than ever, but the interest grows faster than my income. It's like running with a rope around my chest."

Arkad's eyes softened. "Then today, we don't just talk about money. Today, we talk about chains—and how to break them."

The Quiet Thief

"Not all debt is evil," Arkad began. "Some debts build bridges—education, a home, a future. Others build prisons—purchases made to soothe pain or impress strangers."

He let the words linger.

"Credit card debt," he said, "is the thief that knocks at your door every day, and each time you ignore it, it sneaks deeper into your house."

Ben whispered, "And before you know it, it's sleeping in your bed."

Arkad nodded. "And calling itself your master."

A Map to Freedom

He drew a simple chart on a page—no magic, no mystery.

"Here is your sword," he said. "Here is how you cut the rope."

1. **List Your Debts** – Name them all. What you owe. The inter-

est. The payment due. You cannot conquer what you won't face.

2. **Prioritize** – Attack the highest interest first like a fire, or start with the smallest like a spark. Just start.

3. **Pay More Than the Minimum** – Even $20 extra is a hammer. Keep swinging.

4. **Stop the Bleeding** – No more borrowing for what fades. Starve the monster.

Sam studied the list. "This... this is doable."

"Doable is the road to done," Arkad said.

The Echo of Regret

"When I was where you are now," Arkad said quietly, "I mistook debt for power. I thought a new car meant arrival. A sleek apartment meant identity. But I was only renting a feeling."

He looked out the window.

"One day, I woke up and realized: I owed everything. Not just money—but peace, sleep, joy. So I made a vow to owe no one but love."

Ben scribbled that line in his notebook like it was gold.

The War Within

"Debt is not just a financial weight," Arkad said. "It's a mirror. It reflects back all the moments you traded wisdom for impulse."

He leaned closer.

"But that mirror can crack. You are not your past decisions. You are your next one."

Sam nodded. "So the battle isn't just numbers—it's courage."

"Yes," Arkad whispered. "Courage to say: this stops with me."

The Assignment

Arkad handed them each a worksheet, plain but powerful. At the top, it read:

Your Debt Freedom Plan

"This month," he said, "write down every debt. Choose your method. Make an extra payment. And journal not just your numbers—but how it feels to take back your power."

Ben looked at the sheet as if it were a key.

"This isn't just about money," he said.

"No," Arkad said. "It's about dignity."

The Walk Back

As they left, the city buzzed around them, unaware of the quiet revolution happening inside two ordinary men.

Ben looked at Sam. "It's strange. Naming the debt—facing it—it makes it feel smaller."

Sam smiled. "It's not gone. But it's no longer the one calling the shots."

And under the Manhattan night sky, they didn't walk like men bound by shame. They walked like men breaking chains, one step at a time.

Financial Principle:

Conquer debt with a plan.

List it. Prioritize it. Attack it. Refuse to borrow for what fades.

Debt is not your identity—your next decision is..

Discussion Guide

1. Chapter Summary

In this powerful and emotional chapter, Ben and Sam confront one of the most oppressive forces in their financial journey: debt. Despite their progress in saving and investing, they realize that debt continues to drain their peace and freedom. Arkad leads them through a practical and honest conversation about debt—not just as a financial problem, but as a psychological and emotional burden. He provides them with a simple yet effective plan for conquering debt and reframes the battle as one of dignity, courage, and personal transformation.

2. Key Quote

"Debt is not your identity—your next decision is."

3. Reflection Questions

- How does debt affect your sense of peace and confidence?
- Have you ever used debt as a shortcut to feel accomplished, successful, or accepted?
- What emotions come up when you think about your debt—shame, fear, anxiety, or something else?
- What would freedom from debt *feel* like for you—mentally, emotionally, and practically?

4. Personal Action Steps

- Write down every debt you currently have, including interest rates and minimum payments.
- Choose your repayment strategy: **Debt Avalanche** (highest interest first) or **Debt Snowball** (smallest balance first).
- Commit to making one extra payment this month—even if it's small.

- Stop borrowing for non-essentials—draw a line in the sand.
- Start a "Debt Freedom Journal" to record your emotions, wins, and progress.

5. Group Discussion Questions

- Why do you think people avoid facing their debt head-on?
- How does society normalize or even glamorize debt (e.g., credit cards, cars, luxury living)?
- What role does mindset play in staying in debt—or breaking free from it?
- How can we support one another in the journey to become debt-free?

Chapter Seven

Securing the Future

The city wore its evening veil—glass towers glowing like embers in the dusk, the streets humming with footsteps and forgotten dreams. Ben and Sam walked with quiet resolve through the heart of Manhattan, their spirits bearing something both heavy and holy: the weight of awakening.

When Arkad opened the door to his apartment, he smiled as one who had been expecting pilgrims, not guests.

"Welcome," he said, ushering them in. "You've begun the hardest journey of all—the journey inward, the journey of mastery. Now that you've begun to break the chains of debt, it's time to lay down stones for the fortress called peace."

Ben exhaled and sank into his seat. "It's been hard, but freeing. Like we were walking in a storm for years, and we finally saw sunlight crack the clouds."

Sam nodded. "But with every step forward, we see more of what lies ahead. Retirement, emergencies... protecting everything we're building. It's a lot."

Arkad's eyes softened, like a father watching sons grow wiser. "Ah, yes. Now we speak not of conquering, but of preserving. To build wealth is one thing. But to shelter it—to shield your soul from fear—that is the work of the wise."

The Invisible Enemies: Time and Chance

"Tell me," Arkad asked gently, "what happens to the man who builds a house but never adds a door?"

Ben tilted his head. "Anyone could walk in and take everything."

"Exactly," Arkad said. "So many spend their lives building wealth, yet leave it open to ruin—no door, no lock, no plan. They do not guard their future from life's quiet ambushes: a broken bone, a lost job, an unexpected goodbye."

He stood and lit a small candle. "A flame must be protected from the wind. So too must your future be guarded from the chaos of chance."

The First Wall: The Emergency Fund

Arkad turned and gestured to the flickering light. "The first wall is your emergency fund. It is not glamorous, but it is noble. It says, 'I am not at the mercy of misfortune.'"

Ben furrowed his brow. "How much is enough?"

"Three to six moons of your essential living," Arkad replied. "Not for indulgence, but for survival. Start small, like placing the first brick of a wall. Even a thousand dollars can be the difference between fear and freedom."

Sam scribbled the words *difference between fear and freedom* in his notebook.

The Second Wall: Retirement

"What about the end of the road?" Ben asked. "When work fades, and time becomes our only currency?"

Arkad smiled, his voice lowering like a prayer. "That is the second wall—retirement. When the hands grow weary, your money must keep moving. Let your investments become the younger version of yourself, still laboring while you rest."

He turned toward the window, gazing out over the city. "Use the tools available: 401(k), IRA, Roth. Begin early. Compound growth is not just math—it is magic. Time is the ally of the patient."

Sam spoke softly. "But I don't have an employer. No 401(k)."

"Then open your own gate," Arkad said. "A Solo 401(k), an IRA. The principle is the same. Pay your future self as faithfully as you pay today's bills."

The Third Wall: Protection

Ben asked, "And insurance? I always thought it was a waste."

Arkad laughed, not unkindly. "Only the unscarred say that. Insurance is not a bet—it is a shield. It is not for the sunlit days but for the unexpected night. Health, life, disability—these are not signs of fear, but of foresight. You buy peace before you need it."

A Story of the Unprepared

Arkad sat down again, his tone more intimate.

"I once had a friend," he began, "brilliant and ambitious. But he saved nothing for hardship, bought no insurance, and laughed at the idea of retirement. Then came the car crash, and with it, the end of his career. His wealth vanished in a storm of hospital bills. He had built a castle of sand."

Ben and Sam were silent.

Arkad continued. "I vowed to never be unready. So I built my fortress. Slowly, brick by brick—emergency fund, retirement savings, insurance. It didn't make me rich overnight, but it gave me peace. And peace, my friends, is priceless."

The Challenge: Build the Fortress

He handed them each a parchment—this one older, yellowed, like a scroll from a temple.

"Your task this month is sacred," he said. "Build your fortress. Set a goal for your emergency fund and begin. Open a retirement account and commit to a monthly contribution. And review your protections. Are you covered for the storms?"

Ben stared at the parchment. "This feels different than the others."

"It is," Arkad said. "You are not just learning to grow. You are learning to endure."

The Walk Back: Beneath the Stars

As Ben and Sam walked back through the cold city night, something had shifted. The wind still blew, but they no longer feared it. They were becoming architects of their future, bricklayers of peace.

"You know," Sam said, "I always thought financial planning was about getting ahead."

Ben nodded. "But now it feels like it's also about not falling behind."

Sam smiled. "Let's build that fortress."

Financial Principle:

Prepare for the storms of life.

Build an emergency fund, save steadily for retirement, and protect what you've built with wisdom. True wealth is not only measured by what you gain—but by what you're prepared to lose and still stand.

Discussion Guide

1. Chapter Summary

In this reflective and sobering chapter, Ben and Sam are introduced to the idea that wealth is not just for gaining—it's for guarding. Arkad reveals the concept of building a financial fortress, brick by brick, with three walls: an emergency fund, retirement savings, and insurance. These are not glamorous topics, but they are essential to long-term peace and sustainability. Wealth built without protection is fragile. Arkad challenges them to think not just about financial growth—but about resilience, foresight, and the ability to withstand life's inevitable storms.

2. Key Quote

> "You are not just learning to grow. You are learning to endure."

3. Reflection Questions

- What unexpected events in life have impacted your finances in the past?
- How do you currently feel about your emergency fund, re-

tirement plan, or insurance coverage?

- Which of the three "walls" feels most urgent for you to strengthen right now?
- How does building financial protection contribute to your sense of peace?

4. Personal Action Steps

- Set a goal for your **emergency fund** (start with $1,000 if you're new, then aim for 3–6 months of expenses).
- Open or review a **retirement account** (401(k), IRA, Roth IRA, Solo 401(k)) and commit to a consistent monthly contribution.
- Evaluate your **insurance coverage**: health, disability, life—are there gaps or areas needing review?
- Write out your "Fortress Plan": What are you protecting? What future storms are you preparing for?

5. Group Discussion Questions

- Why do so many people neglect emergency funds and retirement savings?
- How does the culture of instant gratification work against long-term financial planning?

- Can you think of a real-life example where someone suffered or succeeded based on how well they had (or had not) built a financial fortress?

- What small changes can we make this month to begin fortifying our finances?

Chapter Eight

The Paradox of Generosity

Seasons had shifted since Ben and Sam first stepped into Arkad's world. From clueless to curious, from burdened to becoming—they had tasted the fruit of discipline, clarity, and courage. Yet when Arkad called them back this time, they felt something different in the air. As if they were about to be handed not just another principle—but a key to something deeper.

Arkad greeted them with his familiar warmth, but his tone held a quiet gravity. "Today," he said, "we speak not of keeping, but of giving."

Ben raised an eyebrow. "Giving? I thought this journey was about wealth."

Arkad smiled knowingly. "And it is. But true wealth doesn't end in your hands. It flows through them."

The Paradox of Generosity

In the living room, a small card rested on the coffee table. On it were words ancient and alive:

> "The generous will themselves be blessed, for they share their food with the poor."

Sam read it aloud, eyebrows furrowed. "But how does giving make us richer?"

"Because," Arkad said, "generosity breaks the illusion of scarcity. When you give, you send a signal—not just to others, but to your own soul—that there is more than enough."

Ben crossed his arms. "But what if we're barely building? Doesn't giving slow us down?"

"No," Arkad replied. "It roots you. It reminds you that money is not the goal. Impact is. Giving recalibrates your soul while expanding your influence."

The Shift Within

"When I was younger," Arkad began, "I clenched every dollar like it might vanish. I thought giving would make me lose control. But then a friend hit hard times, and I gave—not out of abundance, but out of care."

He paused, eyes distant.

"That moment changed me. It wasn't the amount. It was the alignment. My wealth stopped being just mine—it became something more."

Ben leaned in. "And what happened?"

"I started giving more often. Quietly. Consistently. Not to impress, not to earn favor, but to sow life into others. And strangely, what I feared would drain me... multiplied me. Doors opened. People remembered. Needs were met—mine and others'. The more I gave, the more came back—not always as dollars, but always as grace."

Purposeful Giving

"So giving helps us too?" Sam asked.

"Deeply," Arkad said. "But only when it's intentional. Don't give from guilt. Give from conviction. Give to what moves you. Give in line with your values. That's how money becomes meaning."

Ben nodded slowly. "So we start small, like with saving?"

"Exactly," Arkad replied. "Set aside a portion—5%, 2%, even $20. It's not about volume. It's about vision. Make generosity a rhythm, not a reaction."

The Ripple Effect

Arkad handed them a printed list, filled with local causes, people in need, and opportunities to serve.

"This month," he said, "choose one. Give. Not just money—give time, presence, attention. Watch what it does to the people. Then watch what it does to you."

Sam scanned the list. "It's strange. I still feel like I'm catching my breath financially. Giving feels... early."

"And yet," Arkad said, "giving reminds you that you are already enough to be a blessing. You don't give *after* you've arrived. You give *on the way*. Generosity is part of the becoming."

The Walk Back

That night, as they walked through the glowing streets of Manhattan, the city no longer felt like a cold machine. It felt like soil—waiting for seeds.

Ben broke the silence. "All this time, I've guarded money like a fortress. But maybe its real power is as a river."

Sam nodded. "Yeah. What we give might outlive what we save."

Ben smiled, and for the first time, the idea of wealth didn't feel heavy. It felt holy.

"Here's to building more than a balance sheet," he said.

"Here's to building a legacy."

Financial Principle:

> ***True wealth flows outward.***
>
> *Give with intention. Let generosity align with your values and purpose. What you give returns—not always in kind, but always in character. And character is the soil where legacy grows.*

Discussion Guide

1. Chapter Summary

In this heart-opening chapter, Arkad introduces Ben and Sam to one of the most transformational principles of wealth—generosity. What begins as a puzzling shift ("Isn't this journey about building wealth?") becomes a profound realization: true wealth is not measured by accumulation alone, but by impact. Arkad teaches them that giving doesn't diminish wealth—it deepens it. It reframes money as a means of alignment, connection, and purpose. Whether it's $5 or five hours, giving becomes a river that nourishes both others and the giver.

2. Key Quote

> "You don't give after you've arrived. You give on the way. Generosity is part of the becoming."

3. Reflection Questions

- How do you feel when you give—money, time, or resources? What holds you back?
- Can you recall a time when giving to someone else ended up

blessing you in return?

- What causes or people stir your heart and align with your personal values?
- In what ways has your understanding of generosity changed through this chapter?

4. Personal Action Steps

- Choose a **percentage or amount** (however small) to intentionally set aside for giving this month.
- Identify a **person, organization, or need** you care about and take action—give money, your time, or your support.
- Start a **Generosity Journal**: each time you give, record not just what you gave, but what you felt and what happened.
- Pray or reflect on how you want generosity to be part of your legacy—not just something you do, but someone you are.

5. Group Discussion Questions

- Why do you think generosity is often left out of personal finance discussions?
- What are some common misconceptions people have about giving?

- How can we develop a rhythm of generosity even while we're still building our own finances?

- What might change in our families, communities, or cities if more people gave with intention?

Chapter Nine

The More You Become

Ben and Sam arrived at Arkad's apartment with a renewed sense of purpose. Over the past month, they had each chosen a cause to support, donating both time and money. To their surprise, giving had felt less like a loss and more like a gain—a shift in perspective they hadn't expected. But today, Arkad had promised to teach them a principle that could increase their earning potential.

After welcoming them in and pouring coffee, Arkad began, "You've learned how to save, invest, and prepare for the future. But there's another key to building wealth: increasing your value."

Sam raised an eyebrow. "Increasing our value? What does that mean?"

"It means making yourself more skilled, more knowledgeable, and more indispensable in whatever you do," Arkad explained. "The more valuable you are, the more opportunities you'll have to earn and grow."

The Key to More

Ben leaned forward. "But isn't there a limit to how much we can earn? I mean, there are only so many hours in a day."

"That's true," Arkad said. "But earning more isn't just about working harder—it's about working smarter. When you develop skills that are in demand, you can command higher pay, create new opportunities, or even start your own ventures."

"What kind of skills?" Sam asked.

"That depends on your goals," Arkad said. "If you're in a corporate job, focus on skills that make you stand out—leadership, communication, or expertise in your field. If you're self-employed, learn how to market yourself, negotiate, and expand your offerings."

The Power of Learning

Arkad pulled out a small notepad. "When I was just starting out, I realized I had limited skills. So I made a list of areas I wanted to improve—public speaking, networking, and basic investing. I dedicated time each week to learning, whether it was through books, courses, or mentors."

Ben scribbled notes. "So it's about always growing?"

"Exactly," Arkad said. "The world is constantly changing. If you're not learning, you're falling behind. But if you're willing to adapt and grow, you'll always stay ahead."

Turning Skills into Income

Sam raised a hand. "But what if we don't know where to start? There are so many skills to learn—it's overwhelming."

Arkad nodded. "Start by identifying what you're already good at and how you can make it better. For example, if you're good at design, learn new tools or techniques. If you're in sales, study negotiation or customer psychology. Focus on skills that align with your strengths and career goals."

"And what about starting something on the side?" Ben asked.

"That's a great idea," Arkad said. "Side hustles are an excellent way to test new skills and create additional income streams. Just make sure it's something you enjoy and can sustain without burning out."

The Value of Relationships

Arkad smiled. "And don't forget: one of the most valuable skills you can build is networking. Relationships are often the bridge to new opportunities. Attend events, join professional groups, and don't be afraid to introduce yourself. The people you meet could change your life."

Sam grinned. "So it's not just about what we know—it's about who we know?"

"Exactly," Arkad said. "Knowledge opens doors, but relationships invite you in."

The Challenge

Arkad handed them each a worksheet. "This month, I want you to choose one skill to develop. Dedicate time to improving it—take a class, read a book, or find a mentor. And as you do, think about how you can use this skill to create more value in your career or community."

Ben scanned the worksheet. "This actually feels exciting. It's like we're not just managing money—we're building ourselves."

Sam nodded. "Yeah, it's about making sure we're not just earning the same thing year after year."

The Walk Back

As they left the apartment, the city felt like a landscape of possibilities. The lights of Manhattan's towering buildings seemed to beckon them to rise higher, to reach for more.

"You know," Ben said, "I never thought about learning as a way to earn more. But it makes sense—if we're better at what we do, we'll always have more opportunities."

Sam grinned. "Here's to becoming more valuable."

Ben smiled. "And here's to turning that value into freedom."

Financial Principle:

> ***Build valuable skills***
>
> *Increase your earning potential by building improving your skills, adapting to change, and investing in relationships. The more valuable you are, the more opportunities you'll create.*

Discussion Guide

1. Chapter Summary

In this chapter, Ben and Sam take the next step on their journey—not by focusing on money itself, but on the source of it: themselves. Arkad introduces the principle of increasing earning potential by increasing personal value. Through stories and strategies, he helps them see that the more they grow in skill, wisdom, and connection, the more doors open. Wealth isn't just stored in a bank—it's developed in a person. Whether it's mastering a craft, expanding relationships, or launching a side venture, this chapter reveals that investing in yourself is one of the wisest financial decisions you can make.

2. Key Quote

"Knowledge opens doors, but relationships invite you in."

3. Reflection Questions

- What is one skill you've always wanted to improve but haven't prioritized? Why?
- How do you currently invest in yourself—personally, professionally, or spiritually?
- What limiting beliefs have held you back from pursuing greater value?
- Who in your life has opened a door for you through a relationship or network?

4. Personal Action Steps

- Choose **one skill** that aligns with your career or passion and commit to developing it over the next 30 days.
- Sign up for a course, **read a book**, or **connect with a mentor** who can help sharpen that skill.

- Make a **networking goal** this month—such as attending an event, sending a message to someone you admire, or re-connecting with a colleague.
- Begin a **Growth Tracker**: weekly notes on what you're learning, how you're applying it, and what results you're seeing.

5. Group Discussion Questions

- Why do many people stop learning after school or initial job training?
- In what ways can continual learning create both financial and personal breakthroughs?
- How can you build a growth environment around you—one that encourages personal development and opportunity?
- What are some creative side income ideas that align with your natural talents?

Chapter Ten

The Wealth of We

They came not with questions this time, but with quiet victories.

Ben had closed new deals, the fruit of his sharpened voice and deeper understanding of human need. Sam had seen his designs touch new hands, his work traveling farther than his feet ever had. They had grown. They had become more.

Yet Arkad, as always, saw something further ahead.

"You've learned to tend your garden," he said, his voice calm like still water. "Now it's time to learn how to plant beside others."

The Unseen Ingredient

Ben raised a brow. "What do you mean?"

Arkad poured their coffee slowly, deliberately, as if each drop held a lesson.

"Wealth," he said, "is not simply what you earn. It's what grows around you because of who you are and who you walk with."

Sam leaned forward. "So... like teamwork?"

Arkad smiled. "Like community. Wealth does not bloom in isolation. It thrives in shared soil."

He gestured out the window. "Look at the city—glass and steel rising skyward. But no tower stands alone. Beneath each is a tribe: builders, dreamers, planners, doers. The wealth of Manhattan is not its money—but its *people.*"

A Table of Many Chairs

"When I was young," Arkad said, "I believed I had to do it alone. That strength meant solitude. That wisdom meant being the smartest in the room."

He chuckled softly.

"But the truth? The smartest people I know never sit alone. They sit at tables full of voices, each one bringing a different piece of the puzzle."

Ben sipped his coffee. "So community is leverage?"

"No," Arkad said gently. "Community is *life.* It's the net that catches ideas, the soil that multiplies seeds, the circle where vision becomes action."

The Echo of Others

He told them of a small circle he'd once joined—five individuals with different paths but shared purpose. They met monthly. They shared wins and wounds. They sharpened each other like blades warmed in fire.

"I thought I was giving advice," Arkad said. "But I was being remade."

"What did you gain from it?" Sam asked.

"Perspective. Wisdom. And doors I could never have opened alone."

Ben nodded slowly. "So how do we find people like that?"

"You *build* them," Arkad said. "One conversation at a time."

The Invitation

"Start with hunger," he continued. "Yours, and theirs. Seek those who want more—not more things, but more life. Reach out to someone who inspires you. Join a circle. Or begin one."

"And what do we offer if we're just starting?" Sam asked.

"Offer honesty. Offer curiosity. Offer the willingness to grow together."

He paused.

"A wealth community isn't about status. It's about soul."

The Dance of Collaboration

"Two people dreaming together," Arkad said, "can birth what one never could."

He listed names—of partners who had built companies, artists who had co-created, families who had invested as one. "Collaboration isn't just about doing more," he said. "It's about becoming more."

Ben grinned. "Like that saying—if you want to go fast, go alone. If you want to go far..."

"Go together," Arkad finished, eyes warm.

The Assignment

He handed them a small notebook—unmarked, waiting.

"Over the next month," he said, "fill this with people. Reach out. Sit down. Join something. Start something. Let the pages become a map of who you are walking with—and who you are becoming because of it."

Ben flipped through the blank pages and smiled. "Feels like a different kind of treasure map."

Sam nodded. "The kind that leads to people."

The Walk Back

The city hummed as always, but something in the rhythm felt different—as though the streets weren't just filled with strangers, but with potential partners in purpose.

Ben looked over. "You know... I used to think wealth was lonely. Now I see it's meant to be shared."

Sam laughed. "Here's to building with others."

Ben smiled. "Here's to going far—*together.*"

Financial Principle:

> ***True wealth is communal.***
>
> *Surround yourself with those who stretch your thinking, share your values, and walk beside you. In the company of the wise, your potential multiplies.*

Discussion Guide

1. Chapter Summary

In this chapter, Ben and Sam learn that wealth is not only personal—it's relational. Arkad invites them to see beyond solo success and into the realm of shared strength. From mastermind groups to casual collaborations, they discover that wealth multiplies when it is rooted in community. Arkad teaches that the true value of a person is not just in what they know or do, but in who they walk with and grow alongside. Through authentic connection, honest sharing, and collective purpose, they learn that the journey is richer when traveled together.

2. Key Quote

> "Community is not leverage—it is life."

3. Reflection Questions

- Who are the people in your life who help you grow? Who challenges your thinking?
- Have you ever experienced a "circle" like Arkad described—a group that shapes you?
- In what ways have you tried to build alone? What might collaboration unlock for you?
- What's holding you back from reaching out to others who inspire or challenge you?

4. Personal Action Steps

- Use a notebook or digital journal to list 5–10 people who could form part of your "wealth circle." These can be friends, mentors, peers, or leaders.
- Set a goal to connect with at least **3 of them this month**—for coffee, a call, or collaboration.
- Join or start a **mastermind group**: a small circle where you share goals, challenges, and progress regularly.
- Reflect weekly: *How are my relationships shaping my mindset and mission?*

5. Group Discussion Questions

- Why do you think many people equate success with isolation?
- What's the difference between networking for gain and building genuine community?
- How can a community help you manage setbacks and multiply victories?
- What are practical ways to create or strengthen a purpose-driven circle?

Chapter Eleven

Conclusion: The Journey Is the Wealth

The seasons had shifted. Manhattan, ever-changing, pulsed with the rhythm of life. And in one sunlit apartment high above Tribeca, a chapter was drawing to a close—not with finality, but with fulfillment.

Ben and Sam sat across from Arkad once more. The table between them bore the quiet weight of months—journals inked with dreams, plans rooted in wisdom, and the fingerprints of transformation.

What began as a cry for answers had become a song of clarity. What began with lack had grown into abundance—both within and without.

The Final Conversation

Arkad's eyes shimmered, not with pride, but with peace.

"You've walked a path few are willing to take," he said. "Not just to understand wealth—but to understand yourselves."

Ben looked out the window at the city's sprawl, then back at Arkad. "I used to think wealth was something for other people. Now I realize—it's a decision, made every day, in small steps."

Sam nodded slowly. "And it's more than just money. It's freedom. It's alignment. It's waking up and knowing you're building something that matters."

Arkad smiled. "Yes. Wealth is not just a possession. It is a *becoming.*"

The City as a Metaphor

He turned toward the skyline, its towers catching the golden light of late afternoon.

"This city," he said softly, "was not built in a weekend. It rose brick by brick, plan by plan, vision by vision. So it is with your wealth."

He began to list the stones in their new foundation—not hurriedly, but like a craftsman recounting the tools of his trade:

- **Pay Yourself First** – Let your money serve your future, not just your present.

- **Make Money Work** – Invest in streams that flow when you're still.
- **Resist the Rise** – Let lifestyle follow purpose, not pressure.
- **Defeat Debt** – Do not let borrowed time steal your peace.
- **Protect the Future** – Guard the garden you're growing.
- **Give with Joy** – For in generosity, wealth multiplies.
- **Become Valuable** – Your greatest asset is *you*.
- **Find Your People** – Walk with the wise, and you will grow wise.

Each word felt like a chisel, carving truth into stone.

"Wealth," Arkad said, "is not sudden. It is a quiet flame fed daily. With time, it becomes light."

A New Book Begins

He handed them each a blank journal—no title, no lines, just space.

"This is yours," he said. "Not to record what you *own*, but who you *become*. Let it be a map of lessons learned, steps taken, and dreams unfolding."

Sam's hands lingered on the cover. "Feels like we're being handed the pen to our next chapter."

"You always had the pen," Arkad said. "You just needed to remember how to write."

Ben chuckled, then grew thoughtful. “Thank you, Arkad. For the light.”

Arkad rose and embraced them both. “You lit the flame. I merely struck the match.”

The Walk Into the Future

They stepped into the city again, but it no longer loomed—it welcomed.

The rhythm of Manhattan, once chaotic, now hummed like purpose. The streets were no longer cluttered with distractions—they were rivers of opportunity. Ben glanced at Sam, the evening glow reflected in his eyes.

“You know,” he said, “wealth used to feel like a finish line. Now it feels like a way of living.”

Sam smiled. “And we’re just getting started.”

They walked forward—not to escape the past, but to step fully into a future they were ready to build.

One decision at a time. One step at a time. One life, fully lived.

Final Principle

> ***Wealth is a journey, not a destination.***
>
> *It’s built through consistent action, intentional choices, and a commitment to growth. Start where you are, use what you have, and take one step at a time.And remember—the richest life is not just built... it is lived.*

Chapter Twelve

Financial Freedom Action Plan

You've just journeyed through a story that wasn't just meant to entertain—it was meant to transform. The parables, conversations, and lessons you encountered in these pages reflect timeless truths, retold in a modern world where money is both a tool and a test. But inspiration without action is like a map never followed. That's why this Financial Freedom Action Plan exists.

This section is your invitation to begin building your own story of financial wisdom, freedom, and legacy. Whether you're digging your way out of debt, learning to budget for the first time, or preparing to leave a generational inheritance, this plan is your next step. The journey is not about perfection—it's about progress. Small, intentional decisions made consistently over time can create extraordinary change.

Think of this not as homework, but as home-building. You're not just tracking numbers; you're laying bricks for a future of stability, generosity, and peace. This plan is structured to help you reflect, strategize, and act. You'll find checklists, worksheets, and open space to write your goals, make decisions, and monitor growth. It's a toolbox for builders—and you are the architect of your financial destiny.

There are many systems and philosophies out there, but the principles here are drawn from centuries of proven wisdom: live below your means, invest in your growth, build for the long term, and always remember—your money is a servant, not your master.

So take a deep breath.

Grab a pen.

And let this be more than the end of a book. Let it be the beginning of a new chapter in your life—one where you walk in wisdom, steward with purpose, and build wealth that truly matters.

Let's get to work.

Inspired by Arkad's Lessons in The Richest Man in Manhattan

Use this section to reflect, reset, and reshape your journey toward lasting wealth and peace.

1. My Financial Vision Statement

In one paragraph, describe the kind of financial life you want to build and why it matters to you.

2. My Top 3 Financial Goals

Set specific, measurable goals for the next 12 months.

1.

2.

3.

3. My Emergency Fund Plan

How much do I want to save for emergencies?

Target Amount: $______________________

Start Date: ________________

Monthly Contribution: $______________

Estimated Completion: ______________

4. Debt Elimination Strategy

List your debts and your plan to eliminate them.

CreditorAmount OwedInterest RateMonthly PaymentPayoff Plan

5. Retirement and Investment Planning

Which accounts will I contribute to? (check all that apply)

□ 401(k)

□ IRA or Roth IRA

□ Solo 401(k)

□ Brokerage Account

□ Other: _______________

Monthly Contribution Goal: $____________

Notes: ____

6. My Generosity Goal

Choose a cause or value you want to support.

Cause/Organization: _________________________

Monthly/Yearly Giving Goal: $_______________

□ I will also give time, presence, or service.

7. My Skill Growth Plan

A valuable person creates more value. What will I learn?

Skill to Develop: ______________________________

Resource or Course: ___________________________

Weekly Time Commitment: _____________________

8. My Wealth Circle

Write the names of 3 people you want to connect or build with this year.

1.

2.

3.

☐ I will reach out this month

☐ I will offer value, not just ask for it

☐ I will build intentionally, not accidentally

9. My Monthly Rhythm

Create your monthly money ritual.

☐ Review budget

☐ Check savings progress

☐ Track debt payoff

□ Reflect on giving

□ Learn something new

□ Connect with my wealth circle

10. The Commitment

> "I am not just earning money. I am building meaning. I commit to live by principle, not pressure—by purpose, not panic."

Signature: ______________________________

Date: _______________________

Final Word: Your Future Is Waiting

Financial freedom isn't a distant dream—it's a series of daily decisions. You don't have to be perfect. You just have to be *persistent*. Every dollar you manage with purpose, every habit you improve, and every truth you embrace moves you one step closer to the life you were designed to live.

Remember, wealth isn't just about numbers—it's about *freedom, peace, and impact*. Use this plan not just as a guide, but as a mirror. Revisit it often. Adjust it when needed. Celebrate progress.

And above all, believe this:

You are not behind.

You are not disqualified.

You are being prepared.

The richest version of your life is possible—*and you're already on the path*.

Now go live it.

— L.B.A. Tolkings

Read Another Book By L.B.A Tolkings

Preview from *The Purpose Effect*

Unlock the Power to Grow Wealth, Influence Others, Make an Impact, and Live a Life That Matters

Written by L.B.A. Tolkings

Published by Summit House Publishers.

Introduction

The Purpose Effect: Why Some People Thrive—and Others Survive

There is a kind of success that feels hollow. A kind of ambition that runs fast, but in circles. A kind of busyness that fills your calendar but drains your soul.

You've seen it. You've felt it. Perhaps, at this very moment, you're living it.

In every generation, a small group of people rise above the noise. They are not just productive—they are fulfilled. They are not just wealthy—they are wise. They are not just visible—they are valuable. They live on purpose and with purpose.

What is their secret?

It is not luck. It is not charisma. It is not even superior intelligence.

Their secret is clarity.

They have discovered what they were made to do and aligned their time, talents, and resources with that inner conviction. They have, in essence, discovered the power of purpose, and once awakened to it, they live with a force that is nearly unstoppable.

This book is about that force.

You will not find fluff or vague inspiration here. You will find timeless principles and practical strategies—drawn from the lives of great achievers, distilled from ancient wisdom, and grounded in real-world experience. You will learn how to:

- Discover your unique life assignment
- Rewire your mindset for wealth and effectiveness
- Build relationships that multiply your impact
- Take bold, strategic actions toward a meaningful future
- Transform daily habits into destiny-shaping rituals

You are not a mistake. You are not random. You are not powerless. There is something inside you—call it calling, destiny, or design—that is aching to be unleashed.

This book is your map. Your manual. Your moment.

Are you ready to stop drifting and start designing the life you were born to live?

Then let us begin.

Chapter One

The Compass Within: Why Purpose Is the Starting Point of Everything That Matters

Picture a ship setting sail at full speed—its sails stretched wide, its engines roaring, and its crew working with skill and energy. But there's one problem: it has no destination. No map. No clear point of arrival. Despite all its effort, that ship is destined to drift in circles, waste its fuel, or run aground.

Many lives unfold just like that ship. We move fast, work hard, chase more—but beneath the noise is a quiet ache: Why does this still feel empty?

The tragedy isn't in the lack of motion. It's in the absence of direction. Without purpose, life becomes a series of reactions rather than a legacy of intentionThomas Edison failed more than a thousand times while trying to invent the lightbulb. Most people would have quit. But Edison wasn't fueled by convenience—he was gripped by conviction.

He had a vision. He believed in bringing light to the world, and that belief carried him through every dark night of experimentation.

That's what purpose does.

It becomes your fuel when motivation fades. It lifts you when the applause is gone. It gives you a reason to rise when everything around you says, stay down.

Purpose multiplies your energy. You stop needing external motivation because you're moved by internal conviction. Purpose turns tasks into passion. It turns pain into power. You can spot someone who's tapped into it—they glow differently. Their eyes carry focus. Their time is guarded. Their decisions are aligned with something deeper than impulse.

Without purpose, time is spent. With purpose, time is invested.

Without purpose, effort is scattered. With purpose, effort is focused.

Without purpose, achievement feels hollow. With purpose, even small progress feels sacred.

When you don't know your purpose, every distraction feels like a direction. You try to be everything to everyone. But when your compass is clear, you start filtering your commitments with one powerful question: Does this align with what I'm here to do?

Warren Buffett once said that the difference between successful people and truly successful people is that truly successful people say no—a lot. That kind of clarity doesn't come from ambition alone. It comes from purpose.

A person with purpose is hard to distract. They're not chasing every trend. They're not panicking with every shift. They are anchored. And in a storm-filled world, anchoring is everything.

But purpose doesn't just stabilize you—it draws people and resources to you. There's something magnetic about clarity. Martin

Luther King Jr. didn't move a nation by handing out step-by-step plans. He said five words that echoed across generations: "I have a dream."

Not a résumé. Not a pitch. A dream.

That clarity lit a fire in millions. Purpose is contagious. When you become clear, you give others permission to become clear too.

So, how do you find it?

Purpose isn't found by accident. It must be uncovered, like treasure buried beneath distraction and disappointment.

Start by scanning your story. Think about the moments that shaped you. Especially the ones that hurt, healed, or ignited something in you. Often, your purpose hides in your pain or persistence. What burdens you deeply? What stirs your heart? These are signposts.

Your greatest sorrow may point to your greatest calling. The orphan becomes the advocate. The addict becomes the counselor. The broken become bridges for others. Pain, if you let it, can reveal purpose.

Next, examine your flow. When do you feel most alive? What are you doing when time flies by? That's your flow zone—not just where you're gifted, but where you're graced.

What do people consistently thank you for? When do you feel energized? These are not coincidences—they're breadcrumbs.

Then ask yourself: If I never had to worry about money again, and if my work could truly transform lives, what would I wake up every day eager to do?

That's the question that changes everything.

Purpose isn't just about profit. It's about alignment—where your deepest joy meets the world's most profound need.

Try writing a purpose statement. Not for a résumé. For your direction. It could be as simple as: "I exist to help others grow by teaching, encouraging, and leading." Let it evolve over time. But let it guide you.

You don't need to have it perfect. Purpose is not a destination—it's a direction.

And when you start moving in that direction, clarity builds. Opportunities multiply. Life aligns.

Success without purpose is like a beautifully wrapped gift with nothing inside. But even the smallest act carries eternal weight when done with purpose. People who live on purpose don't chase success—they attract significance. Because purpose always pays dividends greater than money.

You don't need more credentials. You don't need more applause. You don't even need more time.

You need clarity.

Clarity leads to courage.

And courage leads to a life that matters.

Over time, your life becomes a masterpiece painted with intentionality. Your choices are no longer random—they are deliberate. Your relationships are no longer accidental—they are strategic. Even your setbacks are no longer shameful—they are useful.

You were made for more than just survival. You were made for significance.

So before you design your dream life or build your brand, ask this one question:

]Is the ladder I'm climbing leaning against the right wall?

Purpose answers that question.

Let this be the moment you adjust your compass.

Let this be the chapter that shifts everything.

The compass is within you.

It's time to use it.

Continue the Journey

The Purpose Effect is available now.
Discover how to clarify your calling, align your habits, and build a life that truly matters.

Find it on Amazon or listen to the free full audiobook on YouTube.com/@TheNextYouNow

Made in the USA
Monee, IL
04 November 2026

67380065R00066